ADVENTURE BEYOND the CLOUDS

How We Climbed China's Highest Mountain — and Survived!

by Joseph E. Murphy

DILLON PRESS, INC., MINNEAPOLIS, MINNESOTA 55415

To Diana, Michael, and John

Library of Congress Cataloging-in-Publication Data

Murphy, Joseph E.
    Adventure beyond the clouds.
    Includes index.
    Summary: An account of an American expedition in 1982 to the summit of Minya Konka (Gongga Shan), as the members battled blizzards, raging winds, and avalanches.
    1. Mountaineering—China—Minya Konka (Gongga Shan)—Juvenile literature. 2. Minya Konka (China)—Description and travel—Juvenile literature. [1. Mountaineering. 2. Minya Konka (China)] I. Title.
GV199.44.C552M568   1986   796.5'22'09515   85-24574
ISBN 0-87518-330-1

Dillon Press, Inc., 242 Portland Avenue South
Minneapolis, Minnesota 55415

Printed in the United States of America
1 2 3 4 5 6 7 8 9 10 94 93 92 91 90 89 88 87 86

Contents

Acknowledgements

I wish to express my appreciation to Marlin Bree for his editorial assistance and to Ned Andrews and Sharon Caulfield, Dana Coffield, Barbara and Doug Kelley, Michael Lehner, Mr. Liu, and Mr. Wong for a wonderful two months in China. The photographs are reproduced through the courtesy of Dana Coffield (pages 82, 83, 86, 88, 89, 93, 94, 95), Doug Kelley (pages 84, 85, 87, 90, 91 [top], 92), and Joseph Murphy (pages 33, 34, 35, 36, 37, 38, 39, 40, 41, 42, 43, 44, 45, 46, 47, 48, 81, 91 [bottom], 96).

Introduction

Inside China, there is a mountain that is a legend. Some call it *Minya Konka*, which means "the white ice mountain of Minyang." For centuries its steep pass had been guarded by an ancient lamasery where Tibetan lamas, or monks, lived quietly, isolated from the rest of China. Pilgrims came here to worship the holy mountain that thrusts above the clouds. Even its name sounds mighty, and that is fitting. *Gongga Shan* is the highest mountain in China. At 24,900 feet above sea level, its peak towers over the Himalayan mountain range in China.

Gongga Shan's slopes are torn by avalanches and scoured by 100-mile-per-hour blizzards. The temperature can drop to 20 degrees below zero overnight. Some say the mountain is still alive, for its icy, steep slopes are continuously being shaped by landslides and earthquakes. It is a fearsome mountain, and it often kills those who are drawn to its high places.

In 1982 our seven-member American team began its climb on Gongga. Though other teams from throughout the world have tried to scale this terrible beauty of a mountain, we became the first Americans on Gongga's icy summit in more than fifty years. We climbed Gongga's icy walls, battled Himalayan blizzards, lived in tents and a snow cave, and escaped avalanches on the great mountain.

This is our story. It is more than an adventure and an exploration of one of the great high places of the world. Our victory was only possible through teamwork, planning, preparation, and persistence. Without these elements, the American team may not have succeeded—or, in fact, lived to tell this tale.

Joe Murphy
Leader
1982 American team
on Gongga Shan

1. Alone on the Mountain

In the high mountain air, I could only climb one step every twenty seconds. Inching my way up the mountain, I jammed my boots, tipped with steel prongs, into the glacial snow. Every other step I pulled out my ice ax, raised it high above my head with my right hand, and slammed it into the mountain. To get enough oxygen at this altitude, I breathed three times between steps.

I had to be careful, for I was alone on "Avalanche Alley." This dangerous area of sudden, roaring walls of snow was about halfway up the 24,900 foot killer of a mountain, Gongga Shan, deep in the interior of China. With each passing minute, my steps moved me higher on the avalanche-prone area toward my team members, Dana and Doug.

I was supposed to find them at Camp 2, where they had been camped alone in a tiny tent for five days, waiting for the weather to clear. As the leader of the expedition to Gongga Shan, my mission was urgent. In the heavy knapsack on my back, I carried a critical supply of high altitude food for the climbers above me.

As I moved higher, the sun continued its run across the flanks of the mountain. Its warming rays softened the snow, causing runlets of water beneath the surface. I pressed my ear to the loosening snow and heard the sound of the clear water. The Chinese had warned us that the snow on Avalanche Alley could suddenly plunge downward—and bury anything in its thundering path.

I found myself in a dense fog that had moved in with the wind. Soon my only guide lay in the bamboo marker sticks left by the two team members who had climbed ahead days ago. I moved blindly upward, guided only by the steep slope.

For a moment, the fog thinned. I saw the marker sticks, showing me the way. But as quickly as it lifted, the fog rolled back in, and I lost sight of my markers. All was white now: ice, snow, and mist. I wiped the drizzle off my dark glass goggles. As I looked out again, my vision was better, but still not very clear in the flat light.

One hour passed, then two, and then three. I lost track of time. The route was steep, with light snow in one place, deep snow in another. At times I detected a hidden crevasse—a split or narrow opening in a glacier—and climbed around it carefully. At other times rocks were barely covered with ice, changing to thick ice in places, brittle ice in others.

At last, I slowly pulled myself over the lip of the snow field. There I hoped to find my fellow climbers, Dana and Doug, at Camp 2. A forty-mile-per-hour wind blast hit me as I cleared the bank, driving me backwards.

Catching my balance, I pushed forward, searching for a marker. I looked about for moments and then in the blank, gray light, I spotted the next slender stick. It was bent in an arc against the wind.

But something was wrong. The wand was not in the right place.

Why is the stake here? I asked myself. *It should be higher up.*

I fought my way to the next wand, which also seemed to be placed wrongly on the edge of a snow ridge. I plunged ahead, but then, horrified, held my next step.

I had nearly slipped over the edge of a snow precipice. Beyond, the snow dropped steeply down the slope. I had come within inches of going over.

The wind buffeted my parka, and my body began to freeze in the cold. My hands were losing their feeling despite two layers of mitts. Above, spindrift—wind-blown snow—whipped along the slope, making it difficult to see.

Was I at the right location?

My eyes scanned the bleak landscape, looking for a tent, my team members, or anything that resembled a mountain campsite. I saw nothing but ice and snow. I felt lost. The wind howled around me. I knew that I was tired and that I needed shelter.

Then I realized that I was alone at nearly 20,000 feet on one of the world's most terrifying mountains.

2. A Terrible Beauty

My adventure on the white ice mountain of China had begun as a mountaineering detective story. I had been a mountain climber for many years and had climbed in the American Tetons, the Canadian Rockies, and the European Alps, and even the Himalayas in India and Pakistan.

During all this time, I kept hearing of a mysterious mountain in China. It was sometimes called *Konka*, which means "place of ice or snow." Eventually I learned that *Gongga* was also *Konka*, and that the translation of the ancient Chinese characters into English is an art and not an exact science.

I wanted to find out more about this strange mountain. Tracking down information, however, was not easy. For more than thirty years, China had closed its mountains to foreigners. It was only in 1980 that the Chinese government had begun to allow a few well-qualified mountaineering teams on its mountains.

I wanted to be among the first of the new climbers in China, but many obstacles lay in my way. Not a great deal was known about Gongga Shan.

I began trying to collect information in public and

specialized libraries. I found to my surprise that more than a half century ago, Terry Moore had heard the legend of the terrible beauty of a mountain deep in the interior of China.

Moore and his three companions were barely out of college when they arrived in China in 1932. On their dangerous journey to Gongga, they had many adventures. They sailed up the Yangtze River in an armored vessel. Later, bandits stole their horses, but the Americans caught up with the thieves in the night and recovered their animals. Whey they finally arrived at the mountain, they were stopped at the monastery that guarded its icy slopes.

"You may not climb the mountain," they were told by the chief lama. "It will offend the gods."

Thinking quickly, the young Americans replied: "We have come from a distant land on a pilgrimage to make our offering to the mountain. To do so, we must climb high."

The lama went off to consult with the other monks and returned to announce their decision: "You may go, with our blessing."

They began climbing the mountain, but it took them a long time to pass through the snowy slopes of Avalanche Alley. Finally they climbed over the main obstacle on the northwest route to the summit—the "hump" of Gongga Shan.

Moore's team reached the top, but at a personal price. One climber had frozen his feet. His toes had

turned black, and he was forced to spend months recovering at the hospital in Kangding, the nearest major town. He had lost most of his toes. Still, all the team members had lived to tell their story. They had climbed Gongga Shan via the northwest ridge without loss of life. Their expedition had taken more than a year.

I continued my research and found that there were some surprising tales of high adventure on the mountain. The more I read and learned, the more the mountain challenged me and my skills as a climber.

I learned that even in milder seasons, the weather on Gongga could change abruptly. A sunny day could suddenly turn into a sixty-mile-per-hour wind with howling snow fierce enough to blind the eyes, tear the skin, or rip open a tent. The mountain was scoured by avalanches. Only in the fall, when the south winds become north winds, and in the spring, when the north winds become south winds, could climbers attempt to reach its summit. To me Gongga Shan seemed a fortress, defended on all sides by battlements of ice and snow. It was a dangerous mountain.

The stories I found about climbing accidents on previous expeditions made the mountain appear even more challenging. For example, I read that in May 1957, the Chinese team had been climbing on Avalanche Alley. Suddenly, with a loud roar, an avalanche thundered down on the helpless climbers. Some escaped the tidal wave of white, but others were buried and one man died beneath the snow.

In October of 1980, an American team also fell before a wall of snow on Avalanche Alley. One climber was a photographer for ABC-TV. The climbers were coming down the alley, roped together in the hot afternoon sun, when an avalanche caught them. It carried them a thousand feet down the mountain. One team member managed to stay atop the churning mass by swimming against the flow of the snow. The others, though, were not so lucky. One climber had broken ribs, and another had broken ribs and cracked vertebrae in his back. The third, the television photographer, had broken his neck and died on the mountain.

The worst accident on the mountain occurred in 1981, during a Japanese expedition. Eight skilled climbers made their final assault on Gongga's summit. Suddenly the fog rolled in. Then the lead climber slipped on the steep slope and, gathering speed, disappeared in the fog. The others began to search for him. Finding nothing, they turned back. By now they were roped together for safety. But on impulse, one member unclipped himself from the safety line. As he stood adjusting his equipment, he looked to see another climber slip and fall. The others, roped together, began sliding down the steep slope—never to be seen again. In all, seven climbers died.

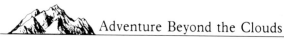

The Swiss had reached the summit in 1982. On the way down, an ice tower had split away, carrying with it the lead Swiss climber. Three had reached the summit, but one had died. Once more, Gongga had taken its fearful toll.

That spring a second Japanese team had also suffered a tragedy. Two from the team were caught near the top in a howling blizzard without sleeping bags or a tent. They somehow survived the night and numb, frostbitten, without food, they began retreating. By this time, the others had given them up for dead and had left Gongga. The two climbers found themselves deserted on the mountain. One climber continued down and was found by farmers. A rescue party rushed him to a hospital, but he lost both feet and both hands. His partner, left on the mountain, was never found.

The second Japanese team was the last before the seven-member American team that I led to Gongga. I was seriously worried about our chances of succeeding on the mountain. I carefully studied photographs, gathered all the information I could find about Gongga, and looked at ways to minimize the dangers. Yet routes that appeared promising lower on the mountain ended in glaciers or unclimbable buttresses—steep projections of rock—at higher elevations. Possible routes higher on the mountain had no obvious entries at lower points. I looked for a way around Avalanche Alley, but in each case the routes led to places that were even more dangerous.

Avalanche Alley was the only good route that led to the northwest ridge, and it was the only route used so far to reach the summit from this side. Every team that had attempted to climb Gongga from the west had turned to Avalanche Alley. And each team had chosen this route despite the fact that avalanches roaring down the alley had buried a dozen climbers.

Time was against us. Unlike Terry Moore's American team, which spent nearly a year on Gongga, we would have only six weeks. But I was determined to go, and so was everyone else on the team of American climbers. We wanted our chance at reaching Gongga's summit, despite the toll the mountain had taken on other teams. We would simply have to wait until we arrived at the mountain. There we could study the situation firsthand. Until then we would plan to use the northwest route, despite the danger of Avalanche Alley, despite the hump, and despite the steep, icy final ridge.

3. Getting Ready to Go

The Chinese were strict. They allowed only two expeditions a year the chance to climb Gongga Shan—one in the spring before the dangerous monsoon storms, and one in the fall after the storms were over. We received the permit for the fall of 1982. The Chinese demanded that our American team send a delegation to sign the protocol. (This was a document of agreement with the Chinese Mountaineering Association.) I was the delegation.

I set off for China on a cold February day. Arriving in Beijing (Peking), I sat down in the sitting area of my hotel room with five Chinese officials in neat blue coats. As we sipped tea and drank orange pop, we discussed the plans for the expedition.

"When will you arrive in Beijing?" they wanted to know. "How many horses will you need? How many drivers? What size truck and what size bus?"

I answered all the questions as best I could, and they wrote it down. Sometimes we bargained about the price of a particular item. At other times they said "No, we can't deal on that. It's in the regulations." And I let it go at that.

The officials liked to bargain, and had a good sense of humor. The day after the discussions ended, they brought me four sets of documents—two in Chinese and two in English. I signed all four along with their chief negotiator. With the signing of the protocol, we had official permission. We could go to Gongga Shan in the fall of 1982. Then the hard part would begin.

Already, we had accomplished a great deal. Our team of seven mountaineers had been carefully assembled: Doug Kelley, a former Green Beret and now an assistant U.S. District Attorney; Dana Coffield, a climber who had just earned a degree in geology; Ned Andrews, a geologist with the U.S. Geological Survey; Michael Lehner, an engineer with Wang Laboratories; Barbara Kelley, a lobbyist and the wife of Doug; and Sharon Caulfield, Ned's wife, who had just graduated from law school. All had trained hard for the mountain adventure which lay ahead.

We had carefully assembled our gear and our food supplies because our safety as well as our success depended on them. Our team planned to take everything we would need to climb Gongga, from snowshoes to sleeping bags.

We knew what lay ahead. On the mountain we would be exposed to extreme cold, extreme heat, dehydration (loss of water in the body), harmful radiation from the sun, and lack of oxygen. The temperature

could vary between thirty degrees below zero at night and ninety degrees above zero (Fahrenheit) during the heat of the day. Reflected from the white snow, the sun could rapidly blister bare skin and turn lips into bleeding sores. The air would be so dry that we would not perspire, even though water would escape from our bodies at an alarming rate. We would have to be careful to drink at least three quarts of water daily to replace the amount lost to the dry air.

Now as the test came closer, I thought back over my years of preparation and planning. As the team leader, I had selected my personal equipment and some of the supplies and equipment for the team as a whole.

I had divided my personal list into parts of the body: head, feet, hands, and torso. I thought about the problems of each and the questions that had to be resolved. Warmth and weight were the critical issues. I wanted to keep the weight of my personal gear, including sleeping equipment, below twenty pounds. From now on, every ounce would count.

My boots would be particularly important. In preparing for my first Himalayan climbing expedition years ago, I had purchased a new kind of light leather boot with a synthetic insole. But the boots were too low cut, and I failed to add overboots or gaiters. The effects of that poor choice of footwear were not long in coming.

At 24,000 feet, with the snow piled up to my thighs and the temperature dropping to twenty degrees below zero, I had lost all sensation in my feet. I did not recognize what was happening until too late. I only knew that my feet felt like blocks of ice. Three weeks later my toes turned the color of charcoal, and within a month I had lost four toes.

My new boots for Gongga Shan were actually double boots with a foam-closed-cell inner layer and a flexible, plastic outer layer. Designed for mountaineering, they weighed less than five pounds and had a lug sole. Because of the plastic, they didn't let in water. Equally as important, they didn't soak up perspiration. But, at $250, my Koflak boots sure were expensive.

Even with the new boots, my feet still got cold. Finally a friend, who is an expert in winter camping, told me that if I wanted to keep my feet warm, I should wrap them in ordinary plastic bags. I tried his advice and put a bag over my inner sock. Then I pulled the wool sock over the bag and put on my boots. It worked. The plastic bag kept perspiration away from the outer socks, the trapped air stayed, and my feet were warm.

Part of my research led me to believe that high altitude sickness was often caused, not by lack of oxygen, but by lack of water. I remembered well my experience on an Indian Himalayan climb. My head hurt, I didn't sleep well, and the heat from the sun at noon was worse than in the Sahara desert. On the flat snow of a glacier, I was on a reflector of harsh, blinding white. The heat boiled up, penetrating my clothing, browning my exposed skin, and burning. Strangely, though I was surrounded by snow, I didn't have enough drinking water.

But I didn't know I had severe dehydration—I didn't even realize how completely dried out I was.

At very high altitudes, drinking water does not cure dehydration. A climber must reduce evaporation of the perspiration from his or her body. I finally discovered a garment that covered the entire body with a material that wouldn't let perspiration pass. The clothing kept the moisture in, which kept the person wearing it from dehydrating. To prevent overheating, each suit had full-length zippers under the arms.

In time my mountain gear was assembled—the latest high-tech, high-altitude clothing, practically out of Star Wars. My undergarments would be polypropylene underwear, and my legs would be wrapped in maroon Gore-tex wind pants. My feet would be encased in the double-layer Koflak high-altitude boots. These were anchored below with steel crampons, or spikes, and wound above by blue Gore-tex gaiters. I had special mittens, a special down jacket, and a woolen cap. My personal equipment, at least, would be ready for the mountain.

On Gongga Shan our climbing team would need two kinds of tents, one for Base Camp and one for use high on the mountain. The most popular and best expedition base camp tent at that time was the North Face VE24. I had read that a Tibetan had unpacked, laid out, and erected a VE24 without reading the instructions. That sounded simple enough, and our team knew that this tent had survived terrible storms. We decided to take two for Base Camp.

That left the hardest choice—the high-camp Himalayan tent. It must withstand winds as high as 60, and possibly 100, miles per hour; stay waterproof and dry inside and out, and set up quickly. Above all, it had to be light, for one of us would have to carry it up the mountain.

Finally, I found the Marmot Taku, which weighed less than five pounds. It was easy to erect, roomy, and warm. Since it required only two pegs, it could go up quickly. And I learned that climbers had used it on Mount McKinley, which has some of the highest wind speeds in the world. We bought two for our expedition.

There was not much left to acquire. We needed special mountain climbing ropes. Unlike other ropes, this special rope must be tested for strength, and it also must be flexible. It is meant to halt a falling body by stretching as much as one-third of its length. Most important, the rope must be completely reliable. I selected a rope nine millimeters (about one-third-inch) wide as the size that would be lightweight and best suited to our needs.

Before I left, I had laid out my gear in the living room of my Minneapolis home. At one end, draped over the couch, was my goose down sleeping bag. Across, on the opposite chair, lay my goose down expedition parka. On the floor, lined up like soldiers, were the vapor barrier socks, pants, and jacket, two sets of polypropylene pants and shirt, the Moonstone Gore-tex jacket and pants, balaclava (woolen hat), Koflak boots, and an enormous Lowe pack, covered with straps. On the

other couch lay the crampons—boot spikes with sharp steel points. I stood back to admire the wonderful equipment that I had gathered with such care over the last few months. It would have to work. If any item failed, I could not stop to get a replacement on a remote mountain halfway around the world.

The second big item was food. This, too, had required detailed planning. If we didn't take enough food, or the right kinds, we could be forced off the mountain. We could become sick, depressed, angry, and irritable. Food was our weapon to combat the strains of high-altitude climbing. Not only did we have to take the right kind of food, but we also had to determine how many pounds of food we would need. With that information, we could be sure that we could ship it with us on the airplane to China.

How many calories each day would we need? This total would be important to calculate the pounds of food required for our expedition. I knew that an average person burned up just over 3,000 calories per day. Hard physical labor added another 2,000 calories, bringing the daily total to 5,000. High altitude climbing didn't change the figures much.

But we would need to take care. If we doubled our rate of exertion, the number of calories we burned would increase by four times. For example, hiking two miles in an hour would burn up 40 calories, while walking four miles per hour would burn up a whopping 160 calories. To conserve our food supply, we would have to go slow on the mountain.

Now, I had to figure out what would be the best kind of food to take. Carbohydrates, I learned, furnish 1,800 calories per pound, while fats have 4,100. By taking only foods rich in fat, we could cut the food weight in half. But who would want only fat foods? Carbohydrates, on the other hand, give quick energy and are satisfying to athletes. Since we decided that most of our diet would be carbohydrates, I estimated 2,000 calories per pound. To provide 5,000 calories per day, we would need roughly 2.5 pounds of food per person per day.

Using ten climbers and 50 days as the time we needed the food, I calculated 500 person days of food. At 2.5 pounds daily for each team member, the total came to 1,250 pounds—more than half a ton of food. To stay on the safe side, I allowed for extra people and time. Fifty days was more than we would need unless an emergency occurred. Also, ten team members was more than the seven we would have.

When the time came to get things done, we split up the work. Doug, Barbara, and Sharon bought the food and utensils. Ned, Dana, and Michael ordered the tents and climbing equipment. I helped where I could.

As we stood on the platform of the Los Angeles airport watching twenty crates being boarded, I breathed a sigh of relief. The routine things had been done. We had our permit, our food, our equipment, and our passports; we were finally ready to begin our journey 5,000 miles across the Pacific to Beijing. Beyond that, deep in the heart of China, was Gongga Shan—the greater challenge and the deeper uncertainty.

4. Across China

In the fall of 1982, our American mountaineering team rode on a railroad train headed deep into China. Our first-class car had departed exactly on time: 11:02 A.M. The Chinese, we had come to learn, prided themselves on being punctual.

We would cross the major part of China, from Beijing to Chengtu. From there we would go by bus and finally by horseback to Gongga's shadows. Then the long climb on foot would begin.

A blue-capped attendant had hustled us aboard the first-class car. Soon a white-coated attendant slipped into our compartment with a hot thermos and poured steaming water over the green tea leaves in my porcelain cup. Outside, on the station platform, uniformed women sold hard rolls and snacks.

The long train lurched and then began its march south over the flat floodplain of the Yellow River. Every few miles we passed another village—compact settlements of adobe walls, one-story adobe houses, red-tiled roofs, and dirt streets. China seemed to me like one large farm dotted with villages. Even Beijing, the capital, seemed rural—an enormous village of two-story buildings gathered together in one place. Only the great square, the ancient Imperial Palace, and a smattering of skyscrapers on the outskirts gave notice to Beijing's historic and current importance.

At the bend in the Yellow River, we swung west toward Xian. We were now in hilly country where people often lived in enormous caves dug out in the hillsides. In Xian we stopped for a day to see the famous terra cotta figures of warriors and horses that guarded an ancient emperor's grave. In the city we watched army trucks, jeeps, and two-wheeled carts drawn by small horses carrying logs, coal, or water through wide streets jammed with bicycles. Every time we stopped, a crowd of curious Chinese gathered to stop and stare at the strange Westerners in their city.

Beyond Xian, on our railroad train heading for the mountain, we were beginning to feel that we had nothing to do but wait. And waiting was the hard part. Our thoughts turned again to climbing Gongga Shan.

"I think this route will be the best," Doug said. He held a glossy photograph in his hand, taken by the 1980 American expedition.

"May I see the picture?" I asked. I had a hard time examining the photo closely because the train was rocking back and forth.

"That section looks avalanche prone," said Ned. "Not very safe."

Route of Expedition
from Beijing to Gongga Shan

SOVIET UNION

MONGOLIA

CHINA

Beijing

NORTH KOREA

SOUTH KOREA

TIBET

Himalayas

Mt. Everest

Xian

Kangding

Chengtu

NEPAL

Himalayas

Gongga Shan

BHUTAN

INDIA

BURMA

TAIWAN

BANGLADESH

LAOS

THAILAND

VIETNAM

KAMPUCHEA

PHILIPPINES

"I think it can be done," added Michael. I noted that he seemed confident of his ability to climb regardless of the danger.

Sharon sat crocheting in the other compartment, her mind absorbed in other things. Barbara was going over the food lists to make sure that everything was in order. Dana said little. He was eager to be at the mountain and start climbing.

As I looked at the route, I wondered about the snow slope up the northwest ridge. It looked long and dangerous.

It has been hazardous, I said to myself. *It took sixteen Chinese climbers down in a roaring avalanche and later caught four Americans, killing one. Only the first expedition–the Moore party—had escaped tragedy on that route. Two parties of three had faced avalanches—not very good odds.*

I shook my head, reflecting on my thoughts over the past year.

There was so much to do to get ready, I concluded, *that there was no time to think about the danger.* I had promised myself that when we reached the mountain, I would consider the hazards firsthand. Then I could see the face, analyze the route, and feel the conditions.

But now as we headed to the mountain, we were at last confronted with the reality—and the danger.

Ned had entered our compartment again and shook his head. "You know what the odds are?" he mentioned.

"The odds of what?" added Michael.

"Of not coming back," Ned said.

"I'd guess they are high," Michael answered, a bit too quickly.

"One in ten," Ned said, as he shook his head.

"But how do you know, Ned?" I asked, surprised.

"I made a study of it," he said, after a pause. "I examined the accident rate on all peaks over 8,000 meters [about 26,000 feet]. And that is precisely what the odds are."

There was a silence in our compartment. A one in ten chance of not coming back—those were very bad odds, indeed.

Dana was the first to speak: "Since Gongga isn't 8,000 meters high, your conclusions don't apply."

We were all silent as the train rolled closer to the mountain. I hoped Ned's dismal facts and figures would be forgotten. But Michael had his own viewpoint:

"You have to have the 'right stuff,'" Michael explained.

"That's right," Doug quietly agreed, "the right stuff."

It was not a good explanation, but it was enough at the time. And yet, I wondered if we were reckless to be climbing at such a high risk of losing our lives?

As the train miles clacked by, my thoughts turned back to how I had begun climbing.

It was as a boy of twelve that I first became fascinated by the mountains. I had fallen in love with the high places of the world—their terrible beauty and the adventure they could bring—as I lay on my living room sofa listening to a radio show. It was about a mountain in Europe called the Eiger.

"Unclimbable," the broadcast had called the mountain, telling me about the most terrible climb in Europe. Someday, somehow, I resolved, I would climb the Eiger. And I prayed that I would be the first.

I began climbing when I was seventeen with an experienced mountaineer. He taught me how to handle a rope, how to set up protection for another climber, and how to use my ice ax on ice and snow. I had read about these things in a book on climbing techniques, but my actual instruction took place on my first climb. My first two years of climbing took place under the guidance of this highly experienced climber.

By the time I was at Princeton University, I had climbed in the Tetons, the Canadian Rockies, and the European Alps. A close climbing friend, Tim Mutch, and I had formed the university mountaineering club.

Even when I was on campus in college, I loved to climb. Early one morning, two classmates and I attempted to scale the university's stone chapel. We were caught, of course, by the campus police. But the kindly dean of Princeton let us off without punishment. He was also a mountaineer.

I went on to do first ascents and pioneer new routes

in the Canadian Rockies and Coast Range. I learned to climb at very high altitudes on Himalayan expeditions in India and Pakistan.

The clack of the train wheels brought me back to reality. All those climbs were a wonderful part of my life and certainly a preparation for this expedition, my greatest mountaineering challenge. I thought how we had all come together as the American climbing team.

For a major Himalayan expedition, such as Gongga Shan, we needed climbers who had a wide range of mountaineering experiences in different parts of the world. Experience was critical. Because the human mind doesn't work very well at high altitudes, climbers need to react instinctively in the right way when a crisis comes. For our team, we also had to have members who would be able to get along with other people. They had to be good team players. Because we were all in it together, and we depended on each other for support, we wanted people we could count on—possibly for our lives.

Now, on my third expedition to the Himalayas, I wondered how well I would do on Gongga Shan. I glanced at my reflection in the darkened train window to see myself as others saw me. I saw a weather-worn face with some wrinkles about the eyes, and hair that never seemed to lay down quite right. Physically, I was still strong. I exercised regularly by swimming, by wind surfing in the summer on the lakes near my Minneapolis home, and by skiing in the winter. I watched my diet carefully, as any person should who cares for his or her body. Chances are I could still work my way up a rock chimney.

A lot lay ahead, but I knew I was ready for my great adventure on China's highest mountain.

After arriving in Beijing, the American climbing team took a side trip to the Great Wall of China not far from the busy capital.

The American team encountered these Chinese people at an irrigation project visitors' center a short distance from Chengtu.

A group picture in Chengtu before departing for Gongga Shan. From left to right: Sharon Caulfield; Ned Andrews; Dana Coffield; Mr. Liu, the Chinese interpreter; Michael Lehner; the head of the Szechwan Mountaineering Association; Doug Kelley; Barbara Kelley; Joe Murphy; the bus driver; and Mr. Wong, the Chinese liaison officer.

A street scene in Yaan, on the way from Chengtu to Kangding.

Terraced rice fields divide the fertile land along this river valley between Chengtu and Kangding.

Children watch the strange Americans pass on the road to Kangding.

Fertile grain fields fill the level land around a farming village in Szechwan. About four out of every five Chinese live in rural agricultural areas such as this one.

The famous Iron Bridge between Yaan and Kangding. Fifty years ago, Mao Tse-tung led his people over the bridge on the Long March to escape from the army of Chiang Kai-shek.

A typical Tibetan home, constructed of stone, on the road from Kangding to Liu Baxiang. Animals live in the first story of the home, while people live in the second.

Beyond Liu Baxiang, the American team members walked alongside the eighteen pack horses for the expedition. Each horse carried 150 pounds of gear. The boxes contained all food, equipment, and supplies and were shipped from the United States.

Hiking up from Liu Baxiang, the Americans encountered this Tibetan woman carrying her child in a Tibetan-style knapsack.

(Left) *At a mountain pass, with Gongga Shan rising majestically in the background, a Tibetan family meets the American climbers.*

(Below) *Viewed from Base Camp, Gongga Shan towers above the mist and clouds.*

(Above) *Clothed in his orange robe, the head lama sits below the altar of the lamasery. He was a boy at the time of the first American expedition to Gongga Shan in 1932.*

(Right) *The ruins of the ancient lamasery stand near the site of Base Camp.*

The scene at Base Camp on a sunny day. All the necessary food and supplies for climbing were carried from here up to higher camps on the mountain.

5. Rising to Gongga Shan

It seemed to be a very long journey. We took the train only to Chengtu, and from there the team and our gear were transported by bus and by truck.

At Kangding we left the Chinese culture and the Chinese people and entered the world of Tibetans. Though we were often only a few miles from the border of the autonomous region of Tibet, our route lay within the Chinese province of Szechwan. Along the way we could see the Tibetan people in their long, wool gowns. They were hoeing potatoes, herding black yaks, driving goats down the road, or washing clothes in the nearby stream. Every mile or so we came to a new village. Its three-story stone houses were guarded by a tall and ancient tower of stone.

Slowly, we wound up the foothills of the great Chinese Himalayas. Our driver, however, made up for the time he lost going up one foothill by racing down the other side. The bus swayed on the turns, sometimes even skidding sideways, and we had to hang on to keep our seats. I began to long for the peace of the mountain ahead.

At Liu Baxiang we began the third part of our long

journey, this time with horses. We had sixteen horses
and a crew of horsemen. They wore derby hats, woolen
cloaks, and curved knives in sheaths. Their animals
were not much larger than Shetland ponies, yet they
were strong. Each carried 150 pounds of gear.

As we rose into the mountains, we walked alongside
the horses and carried a small pack to begin condition-
ing ourselves. At last we were on a mountain trail.

Even here, we entered clusters of three-story stone
buildings separated by winding dirt tracks and guarded
by colorful prayer flags. Crowds of curious children,
women, and men, open-eyed and polite, lined up single
file at the entrance to each village. I noticed that each
person seemed to stand still like a stone statue, without
expression of any kind. I waved, and smiled. Then, as
though a peace treaty had been enacted and signed, the
crowd waved back, smiled, and bid us hello. They did
not move until we had passed. Then I saw the children,
freed of all restraint, dash after us, shouting and danc-
ing; I saw toothless grins of boys and pigtailed girls.

The trail rose gradually, departing from the river we
had followed, on its way to the mountain pass which
was our goal. Black clouds rumbled down the valley,
blotting out the sun and often bringing drizzle. We didn't
mind, for we had the equipment to stay warm and dry.

The ridges of the mountains were all around us, the
snow-capped peaks often hidden in mist. I still longed
to see mighty Gongga, the mountain so high it rose
above the clouds. As I walked, I could imagine centu-

ries of religious Chinese, following this same trail on a pilgrimage to the great mountain.

The walking was helpful. I was beginning to acclimatize my body to the high altitudes. Physically, I was becoming tougher for the challenge that lay ahead and above.

Gray skies had turned black. Rolling clouds had come over the mountains, and bursts of rain slammed down on us. I plodded on, absorbed in my thoughts, and wondering whether the dark skies would lift soon. By evening we had several inches of snow on our tents.

Suddenly, I heard the fast gallop of horses. Through the rain, I saw a pony racing up the hill. Sprinting behind the horse, his feet pounding against the grass, was Michael, one of our team members. The horse had run off, and he was foolishly dashing after it.

Suddenly Michael's face turned white and then blue. As I ran toward him, he began coughing and gasping for breath. Slowly, he sank to the ground, choking for air, but moments later his breathing began to be less labored. I was very concerned. I recognized the signs of altitude sickness brought on by the act of overexertion. Where we were, at an altitude of 10,000 feet, this condition could be dangerous.

We had kept a slow pace on the way into the mountain, to allow our bodies to acclimatize. But Michael, by racing after this wild horse in an attempt to save some of our equipment, had placed himself in danger. He might not be able to recover for the climb to come.

Gradually, Michael's breathing returned to normal. Without saying anything, he rose to his feet and slowly walked around, trying to regain control.

We decided to take no chances. In the deepening rain and darkness, we pitched camp and erected a large tent for the horse drivers. The driving rain turned to wet snow, which covered us and our gear. We cooked our supper quickly and crawled into our small tents.

Finally, we arrived at the end of the trail. Above us rose the ancient Buddhist lamasery that had guarded Gongga for so long. Prayer flags fluttered above us. These were long white streamers bedecked with prayers in Buddhist script, and tattered from long service of praying in the wind. The ancient lamasery was now in ruins.

I learned the story from our Chinese guide. In the late 1960s and early 1970s, China had been torn by the Cultural Revolution. The people, under the influence of Mao, had turned against old ways, closed universities, pushed intellectuals onto the land, and destroyed religious sites. Eager youths called Red Guards had torn apart the lamasery, and the monks had to abandon their mountain home. Now, years later, only a solitary, faithful lama remained. I liked him when I saw him—an old man with a wry twinkle in his eye.

He greeted us when we arrived, and stood watching with keen interest as we erected our tents. He wore the traditional lama's clothing—a lambskin hat, an orange robe, a silver necklace, and a silver belt. A Tibetan knife sheathed in silver hung by his side.

I wondered what he thought of us. We had come so far to climb the mountain that was sacred to him.

Would we violate its holy slopes, or were we welcome?

I saw him move forward. Smiling, he began helping us make camp. I was surprised, but now I knew the lama was on our side.

We unloaded our horses at Base Camp. This would be the first in a string of camps going up the mountain. Next we would establish Advance Base Camp, then Intermediate Camp, followed by Camp 1 and Camp 2—all on Avalanche Alley; then Camp 3, near the steep, snowy hump, and finally Camp 4, from which we would try for the summit.

Each of these camps needed to be set up and stocked with food. Slowly, camp by camp, we would work our way up the mountain. Climbing in this way required careful planning and a lot of hard work, but it would help assure us of safety on the mountain. We could climb and stay at stages. If the weather turned bad, we had a camp to retreat to for shelter. Later, we were to find how valuable this plan was.

6. The Summit Team

Beyond Base Camp the way was too steep for horses, and we had no porters. Yet we had to move a half ton of food and supplies five miles and 2,000 feet up to Advance Base Camp. From there we had to carry our beds, food, fuel, shelter, and climbing gear to the four camps higher on the mountain. Everything had to be carried, one load at a time, camp by camp, stage by stage, along the route followed by the lead climbers. We would establish and stock each camp until our lead climbers were ready to try for the summit. And we had only a month to do it all.

Our team had to be divided up to take on these tasks. Some climbers would find the route to higher camps, while others would carry loads. Everyone, I hoped, would be able to participate, to get used to the altitude, and to have some chance to reach the top of Gongga Shan.

Selecting the advance team would not be easy. Those who were not chosen were certain to be disappointed since the advance team would have a better chance of getting to the summit. The advance team would reach high altitude earlier, become better accli-

54

matized, and be in the best position to make the final assault.

Those who remained ferrying loads up to Advance Base Camp and back would not rise above 14,500 feet and would sleep at 12,600 feet for another week. That altitude range was much too low for climbers to condition themselves properly for high altitude climbing.

"I thought we should agree on a plan," I said as we huddled together, finishing our cocoa and tea. It was now after dark. The wind had shifted slightly, rustling the scrub pine beyond the camp, and flapping the prayer flags above us. Below, I could see a fire flickering against the battered lamasery.

"We've made three carries from Base Camp to stock Advance Base Camp," I continued. "Because the weather on Gongga is uncertain, we should find the route to Camp 1 immediately. The advance team can find the way, while the rest carry." No one missed the importance of being on the team that went forward first.

"The monsoon isn't over yet," Ned objected. "Let's wait until the weather clears and the danger of avalanche is less."

I waited for another voice of opposition, or support. Dana spoke up next.

"There's not much time," he said. "When the weather's good, we should be ready. Let's push forward."

Doug spoke next, also urging us to establish Camp 1 as soon as possible. Michael wanted to move ahead,

too. We were a democratic team. The majority ruled.

We agreed to push ahead with our advance team. Now, we had to decide who was to go first.

"Everyone," I said, "may want to be in the advance party. But two are sufficient. Two can move up permanently to Advance Base Camp [ABC] and then find a route to Camp 1. The rest can carry loads until ABC is stocked."

Pausing to survey the eager faces around me, I chose my words carefully.

"I think we should pick those who have been the strongest and carried the most." There was no opposition.

I could feel anticipation in the air as I continued: "I think the best choices are . . . Dana and Doug."

As I waited, I could hear the patter of falling snow on the tarp above, and the wind flapping the prayer flags. A hoot owl sounded nearby.

"I agree," Michael said finally.

"We should wait a week," Ned objected.

But no one joined Ned in opposition.

"Then the plan is OK?" I asked as I looked around, pushing matters a bit. No one spoke. "Then Dana and Doug will move up to Advance Base Camp tomorrow," I added, as casually as possible, picking up my cocoa for a last swallow.

Later, Michael politely told me that I had chosen well, adding, "My sickness kept me out."

"Yes," I said. "It did."

Our meeting had just ended when I heard footsteps. Peering into the night, I saw the short figure of Mr. Liu, our Chinese interpreter, coming up the path. He was accompanied by his partner, Mr. Wong.

"May we come in?" he asked with a short bow.

After they had settled themselves, I explained our plan. From his coat pocket, Liu withdrew a tattered book. We crowded around. This was the official record of the 1957 Chinese expedition, a book unknown to the western world.

We asked questions, and the Chinese seemed almost casual in their reply. "You know how dangerous the mountain is," warned Liu.

"And you realize how unpredictable the weather is, how treacherous," Wong added.

Wong discussed the route we would be taking and what happened to the Chinese team in 1957. Four climbers had been lost—one on Avalanche Alley, and three on the hump during the descent.

Finally they smiled, bowed slightly, and took their leave. As they turned to go, Liu said quietly, "Good luck."

Two days later, I was at Advance Base Camp with Doug and Dana. I had spent a restless night in a tent on snow-covered ground, tossing and turning in my cramped sleeping bag. We were at 14,500 feet above sea level, higher than any peak in the continental United

States. Barbara, Michael, Ned, and Sharon were below, stocking ABC from Base Camp. Their job was, for the most part, long, hard work.

I dreamed about the hump—or, more accurately, I had nightmares about it. The hump resembles a quarter of a giant orange balanced on the northwest ridge. The face above the ridge is sheer and unclimbable. The opposite side is rounded, appearing easier to climb, but falls steeply away down the mountain's far side. I had been told that if we could get over the hump, we probably would make it to the summit.

My worst fears were of getting halfway across the hump and then slipping and hanging suspended by a thin rope in midair. If the belay (the rope securing one climber to another) did not hold then, I could forget about hanging anywhere. On the 1957 Chinese expedition, three climbers had died on the hump.

It had been one of those accidents mountaineers dread. The Chinese climbers had divided into two groups of three. Each group was roped together.

Suddenly, both groups began slipping on the ice. A climber from one group was able to grab a rock and stop the fall. Another climber from this group shouted to their leader: "Shall I stop the others?"

"No," the Chinese captain said. "I cannot hold all six. Let them go!" The climbers could do nothing but watch as the three men slid by and disappeared forever.

Had the captain made the right decision? I asked myself. *Could he have held both groups to the single rock? Was it an act of courage—or desperation? Faced with the same choice, what would I do?*

Today we planned to carry supplies to Intermediate Camp at 16,200 feet. Then, if possible, we would try to find a route up the mountain to establish Camp 1. I pushed my face out into the cold air, took a deep breath, and then shook the frost off my sleeping bag.

I thrust my hand outside the tent as a way of taking the temperature. I expected the warm feel of grass, but a cold chill filled my hand.

"It snowed last night?" I asked.

"Yeah," came a voice.

"What time is it?" I muttered.

"3:00 A.M."

"That's too early," I protested.

Then I remembered the reason for the early start: to reduce the danger of being caught in an avalanche from the white snows 3,000 feet above us. Climbing early would also permit us to retreat to the protected shelter of this meadow before the sun warmed Gongga's snowy slopes. We had been warned to stay off Avalanche Alley after 10 A.M., when the snow was most likely to let go.

I pulled on my underwear, slipped into my pile and Gore-tex pants and jacket, and adjusted the balaclava (woolen hat) on my head. Then I changed socks and slid into the plastic Koflak boots before emerging into the cutting air.

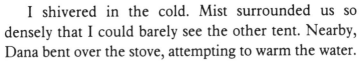

I shivered in the cold. Mist surrounded us so densely that I could barely see the other tent. Nearby, Dana bent over the stove, attempting to warm the water.

I stepped to the supply tent and pulled out a food pouch, taking enough breakfast for the three of us. To start the day, each of us had a packet of cocoa, tea, oatmeal, sugar, and Tang. Doug was now up and ready.

I poured the brown chocolate into the steaming water in my cup, carefully stirring in each chunk. This way I would not lose a drop, and the cup would be clean when I finished. Next I filled the cup with oatmeal, and Dana poured in the water, spilling some on my glove in the darkness. I stirred the oatmeal fully, adding a pinch of sugar. Then I ate hungrily.

After finishing breakfast, we took eight double food packs, plus a rope. Dana carried bamboo wands to mark our route up the mountain. Each of us wore a lamp attached by a band to our heads. The food seemed light enough, but when I added the rope, my load bore down heavily.

I looked up into the dark void. The hour was not yet 4:00 A.M. Gongga was hiding in the darkness and the clouds, invisible to our eyes. A light wind picked up, blowing across the blanket of snow which stretched from the rocks and gravel of a moraine to the peaks far to the north.

As we left, Dana was in the lead, following the same route as yesterday, then Doug, and finally me. We were three solitary figures below a peak that towered ten

thousand feet above. Our route would take us into one
of the most dangerous areas of Gongga Shan.

As we trailed across the upper meadow, I tripped on
the knobs of grass concealed beneath the snow. Several
times I fell, unable to see my feet and the way in the
darkness. Struggling back up, panting in the thin air
and gasping for oxygen, I pulled the heavy pack back on
my shoulders. I adjusted the front straps, righted the
lamp on my head, and moved on.

At the end of the meadow the route began to rise.
The level field gave way to hard gravel and boulders,
which were hidden beneath the treacherous snow. The
white flakes continued to fall, covering my glasses.

I watched the flashes of light from the lamps on
Doug and Dana swing back and forth ahead of me
across the rough ground. Nothing seemed real except
the hard rocks, my heavy breathing, and the awkward
climbing.

Sometimes the mist of a cloud hid everything far-
ther than ten feet away from me. I had to search the
ground for the faint trail of my companions. At other
times the clouds shifted, and the black sky opened up to
reveal distant stars. Then the moon shone with a shaft
of yellow which outlined my black shadow against the
white snow.

The trail went up, over boulders and down unseen
cracks. I was walking, climbing, crawling, and scram-

bling my way along in the dark. Ahead in the mist, the figures before me disappeared. I was alone.

As the darkness slowly began to fade, the deep blue of the open patches in the sky became lighter. A faint glow crossed the valley below. The upper ridges of peaks in the distance glowed in warm light.

In the emerging light I felt warmer and filled with a new surge of energy. I blessed the coming of the dawn. As I crossed the last ridge I saw Doug and Dana sitting on a rock, overshadowed by the wall of a hanging glacier, waiting for me.

Then we were on our way again. We swung into steep snow, Dana again in the lead, then Doug, and finally me. We were climbing close together now.

Our headlamps still burned, for in our part of the mountain the night had not yet passed into day. The footing was much better. Here the hard snow held the impression of the first boot to strike. As the last climber, I could put my weight into the footholds made by Doug and Dana and have them hold firm. But just to be safe, I jammed my ice ax into the snow so that I wouldn't slip. We didn't speak to each other. The effort of moving up was enough to take our energy.

After a time I concluded that even keeping up was too much for me. I had spent three sleepless nights at this altitude and lacked the benefit of climbing higher the day before. I was too tired to continue with Doug and Dana.

After climbing a rock, we tied in beneath an overhanging ice ledge. Below, the mountain slope fell away steeply, cascading down to rocks below.

"I'll wait here," I panted. "You go on."

I had had enough that day. My altimeter read 17,000 feet—800 feet above Intermediate Camp and on the way to Camp 1.

Moments later, they were gone. Small balls of snow trickled down from above, catching me in the neck. I could hear the crunch of crampons in the white powder above. For a brief moment, I saw the shadows of the two climbers brought out by the rising sun.

An hour passed, then two. I watched and listened. Then I heard a faint sound, and I saw a trickle of snow.

Straining my eyes to see and my ears to hear, I waited anxiously. The sound of crampons came. Suddenly, around a corner, a figure appeared.

It was Doug.

"We reached Camp 1," he said triumphantly. "We've reached Camp 1!"

"Congratulations," I shouted back. "Good going!" We were now making splendid progress. I hoped it would last.

7. Escape from Avalanche Alley

People think the mountains are quiet. But throughout the day and at night, Gongga would roar. This noise, we learned, was the sound of enormous avalanches that plunged down the flanks of the mountain to the Minya Gongga Glacier. By the time the roar of the avalanche had reached our ears, we could see that the first plunge of snow had started a storm of white dust. Sometimes a mile across, this massive white wall fell five to eight thousand feet down the mountain. Then all was silence.

I listened respectfully, aware of the danger. I knew that one-third of the climbers taken by the Himalayan giants die in avalanches.

Our goals now were to establish camps higher on the mountain and to supply them from the lower camps. We had to carry supplies from Base Camp to Advanced Base Camp, at 14,500 feet above sea level, to Intermediate Camp, at 16,200 feet, and then to Camp 1, at 18,000 feet. We needed to make these trips without being injured, struck down, or killed by an avalanche. So far we had had good luck, but the odds against us seemed to be narrowing.

Part of our route would be on avalanche-prone areas of the mountain. The worst, Avalanche Alley, had already killed climbers. The Canadians had been forced to retreat from Camp 1. The 1980 American team had not gone beyond Camp 2, nor had anyone for a quarter of a century on this side of Gongga Shan. Now I was off to the third camp, Intermediate, where Doug and Dana would spend the night. We had come down together to sleep at Advance Base Camp.

I set off alone, this time ahead of the others, rather than behind. I searched the mountain above, seeking the easiest path—a line of small rocks, a traverse across a steep slope to the right, and then back up to the left.

As the tents of Advance Base Camp grew small and distant below me, I began to feel the immense freedom of being alone. I stopped for a moment to look about. To my left, I watched a great meadow surge northwest until it met white peaks and blue glaciers. These formed a wall of ice and snow stretching down to the flat land below.

On my first rest I looked back all the way to Base Camp, five miles distant in the center of a long ridge. In the clear light of a cloudless day, I could see the mountain forest. Beyond lay the ancient lamasery and our temporary Base Camp. I thought about Barbara, Ned, and Sharon who were carrying supplies from Base Camp to ABC.

Today I ascended more ably, no longer stumbling, but moving upward with a steady stride. I had discarded the clumsy, plastic Koflak snow boots for my light, leather ones. These swung with ease and held firm, whether in the flat or the side of a boulder. Tired now from the long carry and sweating under my heavy underwear, I kept going until I spotted Intermediate Camp.

Slinging down the pack at the campsite I chose, I refilled my plastic canteen with snow and waited for it to melt so that I could have a drink. I added a bit of Tang for flavor. Then, to complete the meal, I pulled out hunks of cheese and salami from my pack.

As evening came, I prepared my tent and made my supper. The sun had fallen quickly, and soon darkness covered the mountain. As I lay in my sleeping bag, stillness surrounded me, but only for a little while.

I heard a cracking sound, far above; then another crack, less distant. Alarmed, I knew that these were rocks breaking away and about to fall. I listened, all senses poised. I tried to gauge the line of descent, the weight of the rock that fell, and its direction. I could not tell how large the rocks were, but they sounded large enough to rip through my tent and strike me with the force of a falling missile. I recalled how the Canadian climber had been struck down. Too injured to continue, he was lucky to be alive.

But there was nowhere else to move the tent on the glacier.

The odds of being struck are low, I tried to reassure myself. *If you get hit, you get hit. There is nothing you can do. No sense in worrying.*

I pulled my jacket over my head outside the sleeping bag and curled up for the night. Still, thoughts ran through my mind. I longed for my family, and I tried to guess what my other team members were doing. I could hardly believe that I was climbing in this remote corner of China, a country I had never really expected to see. At last I fell asleep.

The next morning I was on my way again. Before the early light crept into my tent, I crawled out of the warm sleeping bag, dressed, and put on my Koflak boots. After a snack of oatmeal and cocoa, I pushed out of the tent into the cold air.

A couloir—a large gorge, or gully, leading up the face of the mountain—was a shortcut to Camp 1. But it lay just below Avalanche Alley.

With utmost confidence, I started up the incline. I kicked steps in the hard snow and ice with my crampons, the steel spikes attached to my boots. At each step upward, I slammed my ice ax into the wall. The ax became my safety anchor. Step after step, minute after minute, and hour after hour, I climbed the steep, hard snow.

But I had made a mistake. Soon the couloir became too steep to get off. My only hope for escape was to keep going up to a spot where I could climb out onto the main glacial slope that led to Camp 1—Avalanche Alley.

Alarmed, I glanced at my watch. I saw it was nearly noon. The Chinese had warned: "For your own safety, you must be off the slope by ten!"

Now I was past the safe deadline, and on the same slope where an avalanche had buried a Chinese mountaineering team. I became terribly aware of the hot sun beating down on me as I inched my crampons forward on the steep slope. I did not even know how to find a safe route to escape.

From above, tiny drops of water splashed on my head and hands. Soon, the drops would turn to small streams, a sign the snow mass was getting mushy and dangerous.

Splash! A small chunk of snow had tumbled down on me, and I looked up.

Suddenly, a patch of sun illuminated the snow above me, and I saw a crease in the wall of ice to the right. I headed for what looked like an escape, to the top of the glacier over ice-encased rock. I lunged, and moments later, I was out.

But my troubles continued. I was now standing in the center of Avalanche Alley. I glanced again at my watch. Now it was nearly one, hours after I should have been off this place. By thrusting my body forward, I headed over the slowly warming snow.

The snow felt slushy and unstable under my step. As I inched my crampons across the steep glacier ice

field, it crackled, indicating that the crystals were soft-
ening. I knew the conditions would get worse under the
sun's burning rays.

I looked around. The snow slope was hard, steep
and treacherous. It was the surface of a hanging
glacier—a frozen river of ice clothed in white. As I
looked far down the snow mass to my left, I saw a tent
that marked Camp 1.

I placed one foot ahead of me, kicking it in the snow
with all the skill I could muster. I had to keep my body
turned toward the mountain so that the sharp front
points of my crampons could get a good bite.

I was being very careful. Any noise, even the small-
est vibration, could make the snow slide. The one thing
I didn't need today was an avalanche.

The slope was too steep to allow me to go straight
down. I could not face out or even sideways. I would
have to face directly toward it and kick straight in with
my Koflak boots. Only in this way could I get a good
hold.

Each step I took had to be smooth, calculated, and
faultless. That meant no wobbling, catching a crampon,
or trying anything I hadn't practiced a thousand times.
I felt like an ice skater in competition.

Within an hour, what had been a brown speck
against a white background became a tan tent, the
familiar Taku. It was pitched beyond a snowy mound
under a cornice—an overhanging lip of snow formed by
the wind. The shelf Doug and Dana had carved out of

the snow represented the only available site for a camp in the area. Below the slope, Avalanche Alley plunged nearly 2,000 feet. I hoped that my team had anchored the tent well.

I began to hurry a bit, pausing less than five seconds between steps. I kept moving down until I was level with the tent, but still some distance from it. Suddenly, my foot began to sink. I knew I was in a snow-bridge—a mound of snow over a crevasse.

The crevasse could be shallow, but it could also drop hundreds or even thousands of feet. I sweated as I sank, crouched with my ax ready. Climbers have fallen, twisted upside down, and become so wedged in the ice that even their partners had not been able to get them out.

I sank up to about my thighs, and suddenly, I stopped sinking. I pressed my foot down. It seemed to rest on firm snow.

Slowly, I leaned forward and bent my body to the snow. I knew that my foot only gave me about eight square inches of support. By putting my body on the snow, I would have a much larger area to support it. I eased my way very carefully to the edge of the snow-bridge. Minutes later, I joined Dana and Doug at Camp 1.

"Here, Joe," Dana said after greeting me. "Ten to fifteen yards from the end of the knoll there's an easier route up through the rocks."

I sat back, letting my aching muscles relax for the first time since early in the morning. I was embarrassed and upset. Not only was I late, but I had also picked the wrong route. Although I was off Avalanche Alley now, I knew I would have to climb here again tomorrow.

We continued to make steady progress up Gongga Shan until Doug and Dana reached Camp 2. I set off for Camp 2 to bring critical supplies to the two climbers, who had left five days before. I was worried because they had been gone too long. Looking down to my right, I surveyed the swept track. It was now steep and icy. The sharp angle of the sun's rays gave the glacial ice the color of a steel blade.

The steel prongs of the twelve spikes held as I jammed in one boot, then the next. I was alone and self-belaying all the way. As I climbed, my steel ice ax was jammed in twelve inches, with a blue nylon cord tied to its head. If I slipped, the nylon cord anchored me to the ax, and the ax anchored the cord to the snow. For safety on the steep face, I placed the ax with care, plunging it into the hard snow as deeply as I was able.

With each passing minute, my steps moved higher up the mountain. I climbed up Avalanche Alley, where the snow was not hard and safe, and passed into a dense fog that moved in with the wind. Soon I could follow only the bamboo wands that Doug and Dana had driven into the snow.

Hours passed as I climbed. The fog was worse now, and I was rising through the clouds. As I pulled myself over the lip of the snow field, a blast of wind nearly blew me backward. Struggling to regain my balance, I began searching for Camp 2 and Doug and Dana.

But where were they? All I could make out were several wands. As I moved ahead in the fog and cloud cover, something seemed wrong, and I held my step. Looking ahead, I discovered that I was just inches away from the edge of the now. Alone and high on Gongga Shan, I had nearly gone over a precipice. *Are the wands wrong?* I wondered. *Where are my teammates?* My body began to freeze, and my hands were beginning to lose feeling despite two layers of mitts. Spindrift whipped along the mountain ridge and stung my face. I could not be sure where Camp 2 was, if there was a camp. Certainly, there was no tent, as I had expected. I desperately needed to find the camp and shelter. The thought crossed my mind that I was lost and alone on the mountain.

Minutes passed as I tried to figure out what to do. I realized that my time was now limited. Suddenly an instinct took over—something told me to stop and look around one last time. Through the spindrift, I saw a hollow. It lay just below the ledge on which I stood. No tent was visible, but there seemed to be a slightly unnatural bulge.

I started down, jamming my heels into the steep drifts. Though the snow was nearly up to my hips, I plunged downward toward the suspicious bulge. I saw that the small mound was covered with snow. As I scraped snow off with the blade of my ax, a dark shining green object appeared. Touching it with my mitts, I was amazed to see that it was a green garbage bag, the kind bought in a grocery store to protect food and supplies.

I tried to paw open the bag, but my mitts slipped on the snowy plastic. After several tries, I opened it. Inside were plastic food packs, the kind Doug and I had prepared at home. It was what remained of our food cache.

But where were Doug and Dana? And where was the tent?

I set down my own pack and began to push the food I had brought into the plastic bag. I hoped I was doing the right thing to leave the food here. My plan was to return to the camp below. I knew I was in need of shelter—and that would be back down Avalanche Alley.

Almost as an afterthought, I gave a loud mountaineering yodel.

The sound echoed back to me from the snow above. But suddenly, mixed with the echo was another muffled weird sound.

I wondered if Gongga Shan was beginning to play tricks on me. Pulling off my goggles, I scanned the horizon. I yelled once again.

I jumped back. The strange sound had returned. It

seemed to come from the snow beneath me, not far from my feet.

I knelt down and began to crawl on the snow toward the source of the sound. Suddenly, I saw a small hollow in the snow. As I watched in wonder, the snow within the hollow began to recede. It seemed to fall into a great hole. Then a dark object thrust up through the snow.

It was a blue mitt—Dana's mitt.

"Joe, Joe!" I could hear. "Are you there?"

"Yes," I replied, completely astonished at hearing my name.

"Come in."

I looked about. There was nowhere to go in. In fact, I was looking at a snowbank in which there was nothing but that small hole through which a mitt had so strangely appeared.

Puzzled, I crawled forward on my knees, and began digging down with my mitts to clear out the snow. Soon I thought I saw a tunnel shape. I began to dig down harder, dog fashion and then I crawled through a narrow tunnel. It brought me into a snow cave.

It was dark inside, cramped and small. Doug lay in his sleeping bag, almost invisible. I saw that his bag rested on a bench of snow, two feet off the floor of the cave. To one side lay Dana.

I sniffed—the air was stuffy, humid, and smelly. Above, in the sagging ceiling, several holes had been punched with the shaft of an ice ax to let in fresh air.

I began to worry. Neither climber rose from his
snow bunk. Both looked tired. What had happened?

Wearily, I sat down on the snow. Doug and Dana
began to tell me the story of how they had come to build
their cave.

After climbing the ridge, they had dropped down
into the hollow to get away from the wind. A twenty-
foot wall of snow rose above them, not quite ten feet
from the cache of food supplies. In the hollow, the snow
was neither too hard to dig nor too soft to crumble.

Doug had felt the snow, scanned the slope, and
remembered his winter camps in Wyoming and Minnesota. There, in extreme cold, snow caves had offered
protection and warmth. Against the high winds here,
he had decided, a cave would be best.

Taking the snow shovel, he began digging down
two feet for a trench. Soon he had carved out a tunnel
that sank down below the ground, angled straight forward into the bank, and then turned up toward the
snowy surface. Once inside, the work of scooping out
the interior cave began, slowly, with great effort at this
altitude. Now Dana and Doug worked together, digging, scraping, and hauling out the snow. Shovel by
shovel, the snow cave grew.

Hours passed, but their determination gave them
energy to keep working as the shadows on the mountain lengthened. Finally, the two climbers placed their

sleeping pads on two snow benches raised from the floor. They unrolled their sleeping bags atop the pads. For safety they punched two holes in the cave's ceiling with the shaft of their ice ax. The holes would let in air even if their tunnel filled up with windblown snow. Then the exhausted pair had settled in for what turned out to be a five-day hibernation that rapidly used up their small cache of food supplies.

And here I found them. They looked tired and worn.

"Did you try the ridge today?" I asked.

"No," Dana replied. "The wind was too high."

"I just came through it," I said. I thought I saw a flicker of resentment on Dana's face.

"The cloud cover makes route finding impossible," Doug added.

"But I just came up through the clouds," I protested.

"You had wands to guide you," Dana argued. "It's worse on the ridge."

I turned to leave. Still, I hoped they would get concerned enough to rouse themselves from their poor state of mind.

"I've brought food packs," I said, changing the subject. "Michael and I will be up tomorrow."

"How many packs?" Doug asked, now interested again.

"Eight or ten," I said. "I've forgotten the exact number."

"I hope that's enough," said Doug, frowning. "We need more food."

"We're running short," added Dana.

I shook my head, adding "See what you can do on the ridge. I'll be back tomorrow."

It was getting late, and I had to get back down the mountain. I turned around and crawled out into the open, thankful for fresh air once again. Snow was beginning to fall lightly. I was not looking forward to my lone descent down Avalanche Alley.

Michael and I climbed apart on our way back up to the snow cave at Camp 2. We had rolled up the Taku tent into a tight bundle and inserted the aluminum poles inside. Into my pack I pushed the tent, the sleeping bag, extra underwear, and extra packs of food.

The route up Avalanche Alley to Camp 2 took me four and one-half hours. This was faster than the day before, but worse than Michael's time. Eager to move on and try for the summit, Michael had nearly sprinted up the slope. A superb ice climber, he reached Camp 2 in a record three and one-half hours—2,000 feet of solo climbing that often required self belay. Michael was an unusual ice climber: lean, practiced, and able.

Three quarters of the way up, I could hear and see him behind me. Then he passed me. On he went, up

and up, beyond the last crest until I could no longer see him. I remained alone as the weather worsened on the mountain.

The blast of the wind hit me at the ridge. I bore into it and plunged across the highest point on the way to the snow cave. Clouds hung heavily over the wind-whipped ridge above me. Even below, in the sheltered area where the cave was, wind hurled the snow over the mountain's shifting white surface.

The unsettling weather was reflected in the moods of the others. Doug and Dana were angry for what they considered our failure to bring them enough food.

Worse, I learned they had not ventured forth to make Camp 3. They had remained cooped up in the cave—tired, depressed, dehydrated, and on edge.

"We have only six days of food," protested Doug.

"That's not enough." Dana argued.

I gritted my teeth.

"We plan to travel light," I managed to counter.

Doug went on. "We need 6,000 calories a day."

"You left out the dinners," Doug went on.

Doug strode off to his cave and disappeared. I put up the tent and waited for tempers to cool down. Everyone was tense.

Seeking a way out, and also hoping to push the two climbers out of the cave, I suggested to Michael a trip up the ridge.

"Perhaps we can find the cache left by the 1980 party," I suggested. Doug and Dana agreed to go.

Their climb on the ridge and my rest had calmed tempers, but the critical issue remained. They would not attempt the summit unless more food was brought up.

That night Michael and I crawled into the Taku tent, while Doug and Dana remained in the cave. In the wind and snow, no communication was possible between the two pairs of climbers. Michael and I brewed our meager supper.

As I crawled into my sleeping bag, I remembered that my pack was outside leaning against the wall of the tent. Reluctant to crawl out of my warm bag and the protection of the tent, I told myself what I wanted to be true: *It will be all right. No need to worry.*

But the wind that buffeted out tent reached fifty-mile-per-hour gusts. At times I awoke, frightened that we might be blown off our fragile campsite high on Gongga Shan.

The next morning, I searched for my pack. I walked around the tent, examined the slope below the tent, and then I scanned the ridge below.

"It's gone!" I said, almost in disbelief. "My pack is gone."

My worries mounted. Not only had I lost my irreplaceable pack, but we needed more food and supplies for a summit attempt. I could only wonder what would happen next.

Then I heard a muffled voice coming through the snow that clogged the entrance to the cave.

"We will go down," I heard the thick voice say. It was Doug. "We'll get the supplies," he repeated, "Dana and I."

It was a noble offer. And I knew what it meant. In effect, they were giving up the first try for the summit.

"No," I replied. "You're best acclimatized. I don't have my pack. Michael and I will go down."

Instinctively, I knew what I had done. The final choice of the summit team had been made. It would be Dana and Doug.

Sharon Caulfield carries a load of supplies over the five miles and 2,000 feet up from Base Camp to Advance Base Camp. In support of the advance team of Dana Coffield and Doug Kelley, the other team members carried many loads up to higher camps on the mountain.

(Left) *Doug Kelley stands in the midst of Advance Base Camp, just after it was set up during a snowstorm.*

(Below) *Photographed from Advance Base Camp, an avalanche thunders down the treacherous slopes of Gongga Shan's Avalanche Alley.*

(Above) *Viewed from above, along the route toward Gongga Shan's northwest ridge, Camp 1 clings to the mountain at an altitude of 18,000 feet.*

(Left) *Intermediate Camp at an altitude of 16,200 feet. In the distant background, the snowy slopes blend into the clouds covering the lower elevations of the nearby mountains.*

(Above) *Using his ice ax with each dangerous step, Dana Coffield climbs toward Camp 2.*

(Left) *Photographed from above by Dana Coffield, Doug Kelley climbs a steep slope on Avalanche Alley on the route from Camp 1 to Camp 2.*

(Above) *Inside the snow cave, Doug Kelley sits in his sleeping bag on a snow ledge above the cave floor. The cave protected the climbers from the fierce winds high on the mountain.*

(Left) *Doug Kelley at the site of Camp 2 and the snow cave.*

Dana Coffield stands before the hump—the huge mound of snow and ice in the background. Coffield and Kelley established Camp 3 at the base of the hump.

Ice ax in hand, Dana Coffield climbs up the sheer, icy face of the hump.

(Above) *Doug Kelley at the site of Camp 4 at an altitude of 22,000 feet. The two climbers set up their tent inside a small crevasse that gave them some protection from the raging winds that often swept over the mountain.*

(Left) *Dana Coffield climbs up the long summit ridge on the way to Camp 4.*

Doug Kelley stands on the cloud-covered summit of Gongga Shan.

Dana Coffield on the summit.

(Above) *Dana Coffield* (left) *and Doug Kelley* (right) *on the summit.*

(Next page) *Joe Murphy, the leader of the American expedition, on the way down the mountain after the successful summit climb. In the background Gongga Shan rises beyond the clouds.*

8. To the Hump

The next day, Doug and Dana began their ascent to Camp 3. They had pulled their packs from the snow cave, stuffed them with food, and had also packed a stove and the extra Taku tent. For safety, they roped themselves together on a 150-foot nylon line.

In the early morning light, against the torrent of gusts which whipped over the divide, the two climbers plodded on. The wind frosted their goggles, tore at their faces and necks, and numbed any flesh that dared become exposed. They rested rarely, moving always upward against the forces of wind and gravity.

Doug led, pushing hard against the gusts and attempting to see the way ahead. He placed wands every fifty yards or so, plunging the red-topped green shafts into the snow to mark the way back.

Dana and Doug climbed toward the ridge that would lead to the hump—that huge, uncertain, unseen obstacle guarding the highest reaches of Gongga Shan. The hump could determine the fate of the expedition and the two climbers. It was the main obstacle between them and the final summit ridge.

Hour after hour, they struggled wearily up the

mountain. Just as he was about to give up hope, Doug looked up to see the northwest edge of the hump, a great semicircle of snow that rose high above. Half moon in shape, the hump's right side was nearly sheer, dropping down steeply. The left side formed a great semicircle whose lower portion dropped away and disappeared below.

Brushing his mitt against his face to see better, Doug made his decision. He placed the future site of Camp 3 just before the hump where it would be sheltered from the wind. It would also be visible so that it could be located in bad weather.

"The hump," Doug said as Dana stepped up beside him on the wind-crusted snow. "We've made it to the hump!"

The two had now climbed higher than the Canadians and higher than the 1980 American expedition. In fact, they had gone higher on this side of the mountain than all but the 1957 Chinese expedition and the 1932 American expedition.

While Doug and Dana waited for their chance to establish Camp 3, the pile of gear and food at Advance Base Camp had grown steadily. Barbara, Ned, Sharon, and the son of the lama, hired for the week, carried load after load from Base Camp over the five miles and three thousand feet up to Advance Base Camp. The last to leave the lamasery were Ned and Sharon. They filled their packs with sleeping bags and left, planning to make camp in the quiet meadow where Advance Base

Camp was located. These members of our team, then, carried the all-important supplies to the climbers higher on the mountain.

Having deposited their loads, Doug and Dana began their descent to the shelter of their snow cave for a second load of supplies. The steps down to Camp 2 were easier and flowed quickly. They were happy now.

Their successful climb to the hump and the setting of new heights for the expedition renewed the two climbers' energy and enthusiasm. They felt good to be climbing again. What's more, they had located a good base for Camp 3. From there, they could seek a route over the hump, establish Camp 4, and finally attempt to reach Gongga Shan's towering summit.

The wind pushed up the side of Gongga, gathering force. Then it slammed west to the crest of the ridge, where it hurled like heavy surf on a beach. High above on the peak, it emerged as a huge fan of snow, curving upwards hundreds of feet.

For Doug and Dana, the snow-blown hump was visible evidence of the awesome wind higher on the mountain. Earlier, the two had climbed back to Camp 3. The next day they would begin the search for a route over, or around, the hump. It loomed large and unknown before them.

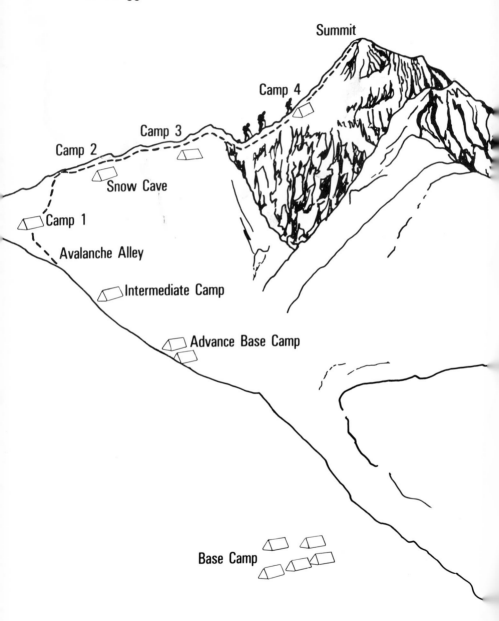

Route of Ascent
of Gongga Shan

Summit

Camp 4

Camp 3

Camp 2

Snow Cave

Camp 1

Avalanche Alley

Intermediate Camp

Advance Base Camp

Base Camp

But now they had to set up their mountain camp. Dana set his pack down in the snow, pulled out the Taku tent, and laid it out on the snow. As he set it up, the high wind caught it, threatening to rip its fabric. It seemed to him too fragile to withstand this force, yet he knew it had to be home for the night. Carefully, he inserted the ultra-light aluminum poles into the fabric.

Spindrift whipping against his face, Doug dragged both packs into the tent. There was barely room for them as the two tired climbers prepared their quarters for the night. They had a brief meal of soup and freeze-dried dinners. These were prepared outside in a snow-bank, over their tiny stove. They tried to fall asleep, but the wind whipped at the tent, lashing the sides with great fury. Snow drifted against the tent, bulging its sides and threatening to collapse it. Through the night, the tent held.

The next day dawned with high wind. Weary from their poor rest, Doug and Dana arose early to pack their gear. They took the tent, rope, stakes, and enough food for four days, no more. At 21,000 feet, their loads seemed very heavy.

The left side of the hump seemed the most promising. The right side, overlooking Advance Base Camp, was sheer and unclimbable. Dana led the way to the left of the hump, up along its steep east wall and into deep snow. Using their steel axes and crampons, the two moved slowly, roped together in case the lead climber slipped.

Ice lay under the snow, and below them the east slope dropped down five thousand feet, curving away and under. This was not the place to slip or fall. They were forced to retreat, and the route across the hump seemed blocked.

Suddenly, Dana spotted a crack that appeared in the snowy mass and inched forward to it. As a veteran climber, he knew a crack could provide him with an easier route. It was a narrow, slowly rising crevasse. Carefully he tested the snow and checked the bottom of the crevasse with his cramponed boots. The snow held. The crack was wide enough to walk in, and wide enough to offer protection against a slip down the the hump's open face. They followed it.

Slowly, as they climbed, the crack narrowed. Dana, who was still in the lead had no choice but to move out onto the sheer wall of snow and ice. Doug took in the slack on the rope, preparing to hold Dana in case of a slip. Dana paused a moment, then climbed out onto the sheer face. He looked down: below him was nothing but danger. Even if the rope held in case of a fall, he could remain dangling. There was little to grab onto on the windswept hump.

Dana climbed upward, his crampons edged into the slope. The razor sharp steel points penetrated the ice— and held. Balancing on one foot, he moved his body forward into space, glancing occasionally through the thin air below him. With a kick, he placed his crampons for another step, then another. Each step had to be executed with unusual care, for now he was in great danger. He had to hold his concentration until he reached the crest.

Suddenly, his body aching with the effort, he pulled himself up the final ridge. He had reached the far end of the hump. Soon Doug joined him on top of their lofty perch.

Before them, to the southeast, stretched the summit ridge of Gongga Shan. This part of the mountain was especially dangerous, and Dana and Doug knew it could be the final trap for them. Here three Chinese had slipped to their death—one of three Swiss climbers had fallen and not returned—and eleven Japanese had died. It was the ridge where the odds of going up and coming back down alive were only one in three.

Dana moved over on the ice ridge, and Doug took a seat. Tired and thirsty, he undid the luncheon pack and pulled out chunks of cheese and salami to share. As they ate, the solid food began to renew their strength. Still, the two did not speak of the decision which they must make.

Both knew now that they were faced with two choices: to return to Camp 2, or to attempt the summit. The awfulness of the decision weighed heavily on their minds. When they crossed the hump, there would be no turning back. They would have to set up Camp 4, if they could, and the next day, ascend to the summit.

Their timetable was well defined. If they went on, they had one day to make it all the way to the top. After that, they would exhaust the critical rations.

"Shall we try it?" Doug spoke first.

A moment passed before Dana answered.

"Let's go for it."

9. To the Summit

From where the two climbers stood, the far side of the hump plunged to a notch in the ridge. On either side of the notch, the walls of the mountain dropped into space. The light was fading fast. They had to descend.

Doug adjusted the nylon line for a belay. Dana started carefully down the sheer face, plunging his crampons into the deep snow. He needed a straight descent that would drop him directly to the center of the notch. Down he moved—twenty feet, fifty, one hundred. Suddenly, the rope jerked tight. He had another fifty feet to go, but all the rope was out.

The notch was too far down for the 150-foot rope to reach. Beyond its reach no belay was possible.

"Off belay," Dana yelled, and the two moved together—without protection. A slip now could be fatal. Suddenly, the steep snow ended.

Dana had reached the saddle. Beyond, the slope angled up like a flat iron tipped on edge. The ridge swirled in the snow driven up from winds below. The slope was steep, and the going was hard.

In the remaining hours of the day, Dana and Doug knew they had to climb as high as they could to shorten

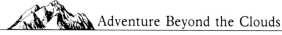

the distance for their summit attempt. Worse, somehow they had to find a site for Camp 4 on this steep ridge.

There must be one, Dana thought. *There must be at least one flat place on this steep ridge large enough to hold our tent.*

They moved upward, a halting step at a time—a hundred feet, two hundred, three hundred. At this altitude—22,000 feet—they breathed several times before each tiring step.

The light began to fade. Desperately, Dana searched the slope. Suddenly, he saw a low place that might serve as protection against the driving wind. Cutting down and slightly to the left, he pushed his boots into the sinking snow. As he came closer, he could see a small crevasse. It had an opening that might be large enough to hold the Taku tent. Inside it they would be out of the worst of the ever-present, driving wind.

The two dropped their packs and removed the tent. Working together in the fading light and wind, they spread it out on the snow within the small crevasse. It fit! When the tent was erected, they could see that the top barely stuck above the surface of the snow.

The protection was welcome, but they realized that this site for Camp 4 might be a mixed blessing. Dana wondered if they could find the tent the next day when they returned from their try for the summit. He worried that they might be nearing exhaustion and arrive when the light was fading. The two climbers chose to take that risk.

They counted their precious food packs, and this, too, was critical. Two days of food supplies had been used, which meant that only three days of food remained. That was enough to climb to the summit and return, but no more.

That night the wind swept over and around the tent in its hole on the high ridge of the mountain. Tomorrow they would attempt the most dangerous part of their climb. As they tried to rest, each man had his own thoughts. Dana wondered what Ned and Sharon were doing and where the rest of the team was on the mountain. Doug thought about his wife, Barbara, whom he missed so much. Would he see her again? For a moment he wondered, and then he brushed aside the disturbing thought. As the wind clawed at their tent, it seemed as if the mountain were alive and jealous of its lofty, solitary majesty.

The tent was quiet in the morning. There was no evidence of the terrible wind that they had struggled against on each of the preceding days. Doug crawled out into a clear, calm day and smiled. The change on Gongga could be a good sign. They needed a windless day, for they did not have enough food to postpone the summit attempt.

Dana pulled his overboots on, strapped on his crampons, stood up, and tied himself to the nylon climbing rope. He placed only bamboo marker wands and a light

lunch in his pack. *No heavy food today,* he thought. *Today is summit day!*

He took two quick steps forward, then stopped, panting. He could feel his energy drop, a reminder of the thin air at 22,000 feet above sea level. Doug came out, secured himself to the rope, and the two readied themselves for the ascent. Dana started up first while Doug played out the line through his heavy mitts. The sky was blue, with not a cloud in sight.

The effort of putting one foot above the other while searching for the right route took all of Dana's concentration. Soon the route turned into steep, wind-crusted ice and snow. Aware of their limited time to get to the summit and back, Dana and Doug began pushing themselves hard.

As they rose, the day remained clear and still. The conditions eased the climbing, saving valuable time and energy. The two climbers were approaching 24,000 feet—less than 1,000 feet below the summit. Above, the landscape was filled with strange, threatening formations of snow.

Dana became tired after 2,500 feet of lead climbing up the final summit ridge. Around three in the afternoon, Doug took over the lead. He began to search for a way to the summit. He moved to the right, up a band of slippery ice-covered rock, and found the climbing tricky on the steep face. Ice on rock was always a special danger.

A half hour later, Doug and Dana knew their time

was running out. The sun began to drop, and clouds began to roll in toward Gongga Shan. The climbers were concerned because cloud cover could be like a fog on the mountain. It increased the risk of getting lost, of not reaching the summit, and of not being able to find the tent later.

Perhaps we should turn back, Doug thought. Climbing in the poor visibility and fading light became more dangerous with each passing minute.

Yet he kept moving, at times tugging at the rope to encourage his partner along. Though he was bone weary, he wanted to move faster. He knew they had to reach the summit with enough time left to get back to their tent 3,000 feet below.

Drifting clouds closed in on the anxious climbers, and soon all was white. The sharp images of the ridge line merged into the thick haze. They continued, feeling they were near the top, but not knowing for sure.

On they moved, toward the next hump, lifting one knee and boot, and then the other. They counted between each painful step. *Can I make it?* Doug wondered. *Can I do just one more step?*

Drawing on his last reserves of strength, Doug pushed on to the next ridge. Finally, he heaved his weight up and over in a last effort. The air was now so thin that every effort used up energy-giving oxygen.

Dana followed on the rope below. He was nearly exhausted from the long lead, and almost blind in the mist which swirled around him.

Suddenly, in the mist they could see nothing above them. The mountain sloped down on all sides—they could climb no higher. They were atop Gongga Shan's summit.

But even as they recognized their success, they wondered if they had made it in time. Already, Doug and Dana saw that long shadows had begun to linger over the Himalayas.

10. Danger on the Summit

They were weary—incredibly weary. They had to rest, but they also had a brief ceremony to perform. Dana photographed Doug, who crouched on the small snow summit. He held two small flags, a red Chinese flag that had been sewn at the last minute by Liu, and the red, white, and blue American flag that they had carried so far for this moment. Then Doug recorded the scene while Dana posed. After that, too tired to speak, each climber swallowed a few morsels of half-frozen food.

Suddenly alarmed, Dana glanced at his wristwatch. It was 4:30 P.M. He realized with a start that they had rested on the summit for a full thirty minutes and had only three hours of daylight left. Since the climb had already taken more than six hours, he knew they had to get off the summit and back to the tent at Camp 4.

All of Dana's instincts cried out to hurry down the mountain. *If we don't get to the tent in time to find it,* he worried, *we will die of exposure.* At this elevation on the high flanks of the mountain, and exposed to a high wind, he and Doug would stand little chance of survival without the shelter of a tent. Exposure on Gongga was to be avoided at all costs.

Doug became concerned for another reason. He knew time was against them, but his main concern was not to slip. He remembered that the two preceding expeditions, the Chinese and the Swiss, had lost climbers on the return from the summit. Three of the Chinese fell on the way down. One of the Swiss plunged to his death when the ice tower he was holding broke off. Doug, too, was as tired as they must have been. He resolved to exercise great caution—and go slow.

As they departed from the summit at half-past four in the afternoon, each climber had a different plan on how to go down. Dana wanted speed, while Doug wanted caution. Already their problems were beginning to mount. Moving down, they encountered dense clouds blanketing the mountain. Worse, the cold was increasing, and the light continued to fade. The wands they had placed in the snow to mark their route were hard to spot.

Dana led the way, pushing his boots down. He was dead tired, but determined to get down as fast as possible. As he moved, the rope connecting the two climbers yanked at Doug.

"Not so fast," shouted Doug. "I don't want to slip."

"We've got to get down," Dana replied, anxious to descend.

Bound together by the same rope, they could only move in a united, cooperative effort. Doug, who anchored Dana by the rope, soon found himself in control. Dana kept moving quickly, while Doug restrained him from the rear.

This must have been where the Chinese fell, Doug thought. *Care is essential,* he repeated to himself. *We don't want to repeat the Chinese mistake.*

Below the ice, Dana moved his boots onto the hard snow, searching for the next wand. On this immense peak in the growing darkness, he did not want to wander off in the wrong direction or fall through an unseen cornice.

After six that evening, faint shadows lengthened in the snow. Weird shapes appeared in the distance. Dana could hardly make out the notch or the hump where their tent and food were secured.

Now he had difficulty seeing where to place his crampons. His legs felt so heavy that he found making a step nearly impossible. He was nearing complete exhaustion. He also realized that he had a tendency to fall.

But he pushed forward, afraid to be exposed on the mountain at night without a sleeping bag or a tent. He knew they could not survive alone.

We have to find the tent! he kept repeating to himself.

His bloodshot eyes searched for the next wand and, finding it, sought the next. But now darkness set in, creating the situation Dana feared most. Time had run out on the mountain—and he could not find the wand that would lead him back to the tent.

Dana's search had failed. At Doug's suggestion, the two men halted, sat down in the snow, and tried to figure out where they were and where the tent might be. The hour was well after eight.

Once again, Dana moved ahead, searching the snow mass. Almost at the last instant, he saw a faint object outlined against the snow.

Could it be? he thought to himself.

He pushed his hand out, trying to touch what he could not see. He felt something hard in the snow. The wand!

Dana looked up, and, straining to see, he recognized the familiar outline of their Taku tent. It was just six feet away from him.

"It's here!" he shouted, turning toward Doug in the distance, "I've found the tent!"

Shakily, he fell on his knees before the tent and crawled inside. Doug followed. As they collapsed on their sleeping bags, the two American climbers knew, for the first time, that the odds had changed. They now had a chance of coming down from the summit of Gongga Shan alive.

The next morning, the two climbers took down their tent, filled their packs, roped up, and set off toward the notch. In their happy frame of mind, they worried only about their ability to climb up the far side of the hump.

First Doug took the lead, and then Dana led the way up the wall of the hump, now deep in snow. When the rope played out, the two climbed with nothing to guard against a fall.

For a while, Dana doubted his ability to climb to the top of the hump. He moved over the steep right face, climbing in an endless wall of snow. He kept plunging his feet into the white crystals until he finally saw the upper lip of the hump beneath his feet.

Made it, he thought, rejoicing and plunging his ax forward into the snow. Now, he believed, nothing could stop them. But he began to worry about the other members of the team.

Dana and Doug pushed on past the site of Camp 3 and down the ridge. They climbed through strange formations to search out the wands, which were frosted and half hidden in the snow.

After turning down the main ridge toward the snow cave, they stumbled wearily into Camp 2. When they arrived, they expected it to be empty. Instead, they were astounded to see a small figure, bent in the wind, coming toward them. It was Michael.

Face grizzled with a beard, his eyes bloodshot, Michael showed the ill effects of two nights of sleeping exposed. Unable to find the tent or the cave, he had slept in a sack open to the elements 20,000 feet above sea level.

"We made it," blurted out Doug.

"What are you doing here?" Dana asked, amazed.

"Waiting for you," Michael replied. "I couldn't find the tent."

"We cached it in a crevasse," Doug explained, "so it wouldn't blow away." He glanced about for a moment. "The snow cave is buried?"

Michael nodded.

"Why didn't you wait for me?" Michael asked, frowning.

"You were late," Doug said slowly. "We thought we'd better go for it."

Michael seemed to lean forward a little, his face draining white.

"I want to try solo!" he exclaimed.

"You can't. We're exhausted. We'll need your help to get down," Doug said. "We can't get back without you."

11. Sharing the Victory

The mist that filled the meadow was so thick that I could barely see Sharon's face ten feet away. We sat near the stove at Advance Base Camp, each with the same question on our minds. What was taking place high up on the mountain?

Suddenly we heard a sound from above.

"I think I hear voices," I said.

"I thought I saw someone on the ridge two days ago," Barbara added, looking upward and listening. "It could have been Doug or Dana."

I started off into the mist toward the sounds. Barbara went in another direction, and Sharon in a third.

As I stumbled over the thick clumps of grass, I heard voices again.

"Michael, Doug, Dana," I called.

Then I heard Barbara shouting, "Doug, Doug."

Suddenly, I saw a thin figure coming toward me, and I recognized him.

"Dana," I repeated, "Are all of you here?"

"We're OK. We're all here," he replied.

In a few minutes we gathered to hear the news.

A tired Dana spoke. "We made it," he said simply. "We made the summit."

The Buddhist prayer flags flapped in the breeze. High above, the summit of Gongga Shan thrust upward into the bright, sunlit sky. Below, the waters from Gongga's glacier rushed away through the forest. I could see the trail that led back to Liu Baxiang, from which we had come nearly two months earlier. As the shadows of late afternoon darkened the forest, I followed the trail down from Base Camp to see the head lama one last time.

He was dressed in a sheepskin coat, silver belt, and fur hat. His round, yellow face beamed as we shook hands. He clasped me by the arm and a gentle smile spread on his face. We sat down together for our last talk. There was so much I wanted to understand.

"Were you here for the first expedition?" I asked.

Slowly, the lama replied, selecting his words with care.

"When I was a boy, I stood in the trail and watched two men ride up this path to the lamasery—the most sacred in China.

"The faces of the riders were white. They were not Tibetan, not Chinese. They spoke a strange language. When they approached the chief lama, they spoke slowly and gestured with their hands.

"Later, two other men came. One was white, the other Chinese. I watched them go down the valley. They followed the river to the mountain."

The lama looked up at Gongga Shan and then continued.

"They did not come back for two months. Then I heard they had climbed the holy peak, Gongga, and reached the summit. When news of the ascent came, excitement was very great.

"Like those long before, you've gone high on the holy mountain. It brings back memories. And, once again, much excitement."

The lama paused, and then continued. "You have treated us well."

A few days later, it was time to leave. The sun shone through the trees, casting a soft shade of green on everything it touched. The snow of former days had melted. All of us seemed happy to be going.

I watched the Tibetans and the Chinese line up to bid us good-bye. There was the photographer, the cheery Chinese, and finally the lama himself.

As we trudged down the path, we shook hands with each well-wisher. Finally, I stood before the lama. He grasped my arm strongly and held up his thumb, a broad smile on his face.

"Tong gi," he said.

"Tong gi," I replied, and then added in English, "Good-bye."

As I glanced down the trail in the sunlight, I thought about what we had accomplished. Two of us, Dana and Doug, had reached the summit of Gongga Shan. The expedition had succeeded without loss or injury of any member. No other expedition could make this claim—neither the original American party, the Chinese, the Swiss, nor any of the recent teams who had lost members in unsuccessful attempts. For the Chinese, that was our greatest accomplishment—the summit gained without accident or death.

I looked back one final time to see Gongga towering over us in silent majesty. I saw the lama, in his orange robe, now waving both arms and smiling. As I watched, the memories flooded back, and I knew then that none of us would ever forget our adventure beyond the clouds.

Appendix A
A Note for Young Climbers

Because there were no climbing schools when I started, I learned from books and while climbing mountains with an experienced climber. Now there are good climbing schools in most parts of the country where instructors teach how to climb different kinds of rock and snow. They also teach safety techniques such as belaying, or protecting a climbing partner by securing a rope tied to the climber.

If you attend a climbing school, apply the lessons you are taught and use good judgement. Using the skills learned in such a school, you can safely climb local routes. It's challenging and fun.

For major mountains, a climber needs more experience than he or she can gain on local routes. First, you need to climb with experienced persons so that you learn how to handle large mountains: how to find routes, how to read the weather, when to turn back, what to do under the various conditions you encounter. By climbing in different mountain areas with experienced climbers, you build up your own level of experience and ability.

If you are interested in learning to climb mountains, courses are offered by high schools and colleges and by outdoor programs such as National Outdoor Leadership School and Outward Bound. In addition, there are a number of schools that specialize in teaching mountaineering. A few of the major schools are listed below. Many are open only during the summer months.

American Alpine Institute & North Cascades Alpine School
1212 24th Street, Bellingham, WA 98225
Phone: (206) 671-1505

Colorado Mountain School
Box 2106, Estes Park, CO 80517
Phone: (303) 586-5758

EMS Climbing School
Main Street, North Conway, NH 03860
Phone: (603) 356-5433
1428 15th Street, Denver, CO 80202
Phone: (303) 571-1160

Exum Mountain Guides
Grand Teton National Park
Box 56, Moose, WY 83012
Phone: (307) 733-2297

International Mountain Climbing School, Inc.
Box 239, Conway, NH 03818
Phone: (603) 447-6700

The Mountaineering School at Vail, Inc.
P.O. Box 3034, Vail, CO 81658
Phone: (303) 476-4123

Nantahala Outdoor Center
U.S. 19 West, Box 41, Bryson City, NC 28713
Phone: (704) 488-2175

Palisade School of Mountaineering
P.O. Box 694, Bishop, CA 93514
Phone: (619) 873-5037

Rainier Mountaineering, Inc.
Paradise, WA 98398
Phone: (206) 569-2227

Seneca Rock Climbing School
P.O. Box 53, Seneca Rock, WV 26884
Phone: (304) 567-2600

Yosemite Mountaineering School
Yosemite National Park, CA 95389
Phone: (209) 372-1000

Appendix B
The Gongga Shan Time Line

1932

September   American team makes first ascent of Gongga Shan via northwest ridge

1957

May   Chinese make second ascent; four climbers lost

1979

July   First plans made for future expedition to China

1980

28 April   Application submitted to Chinese for a 1981 expedition to Gongga Shan

23 June   Application accepted for Northwest Ridge climb in fall 1982

October   Two American expeditions fail to climb Gongga Shan from northwest; one climber killed

1981

15 January   Peak fee paid to confirm booking for expedition

13 February	Murphy negotiates with Chinese officials; signs protocol in Beijing
10 May	Japanese expedition fails and loses seven climbers
	Swiss expedition fails to climb Gongga Shan
21 September	Team completed (Andrews, Caulfield, Coffield, Lehner, B. Kelley, D. Kelley, and Murphy)

1982

9 February	Deposit paid (20 per cent of estimated costs to Chinese Mountaineering Association as agreed in protocol
Spring	Swiss expedition makes third ascent; one climber lost
May	Canadian expedition fails; one climber injured
21 May	Japanese expedition fails on northeast ridge; one climber lost, one found after nineteen-day ordeal
1 September	Depart from Los Angeles by plane
3 September	Arrive Beijing
6 September	Take train from Beijing to Chengtu
11 September	Drive from Chengtu to Yaan
12 September	Drive from Yaan to Kangding
13 September	Drive from Kangding to Liu Baxiang
14 September	Horses and team departs from Liu Baxiang

16 September	Gear and full party arrive at Base Camp, established next to lamasery at 12,600-foot altitude
19 September	Advance Base Camp (14,500 feet) established
23 September	Intermediate Camp (16,200 feet) occupied
24 September	Camp 1 (18,000 feet) occupied by Coffield and Doug Kelley; others move food and equipment up to lower camps
26 September	Camp 2 (19,200 feet) established with snow cave just below crest of north-west ridge and above Avalanche Alley
28 September	Caulfield and Andrews move permanently to Advance Base Camp, joining Barbara Kelley
29 September	Four climbers at Camp 2; high winds
30 September	Murphy and Lehner return to Advance Base Camp for more supplies
1 October	Coffield and Doug Kelley occupy Camp 3 (20,800 feet) just below the hump
2 October	Hump crossed and Camp 4 (22,000 feet) set up on final summit ridge
3 October	Coffield and Kelley reach summit
4 October	Summit team removes high camps and recrosses hump to Camp 2 where they find Lehner

5 October	Entire team back together at Advance Base Camp
8 October	Murphy and Andrews make first ascent of Nochma (18,790 feet); others follow the next day
10 October	Coffield and Lehner make first ascent of Gomba (18,820 feet); Murphy and Andrews follow two days later
14 October	Advance Base Camp dismantled
18 October	Base Camp abandoned
20 October	Begin drive from Liu Baxiang to Chengtu
22 October	Return to Chengtu
23-4 October	Chengtu-Beijing by train
25-6 October	Negotiations with Chinese officials
27 October	Leave Beijing for home
28 October	Arrive San Francisco

Glossary

ABC—Advance Base Camp, a forward base camp located closer to the summit of the mountain than Base Camp

acclimatize—to condition the body to function effectively at high altitudes; one guideline often used is for climbers to gain no more than 1,000 feet per day in altitude above 15,000 feet (measured by the elevation at which climbers sleep)

altimeter—an instrument for measuring altitude

balaclava—a warm woolen hat

Base Camp—the lowest permanent camp of climbing expedition

belay—to prevent a climber from falling by securing the rope tied to him to another climber or to a piton (a spike that is driven into a rock or ice surface as a support and often has an eye for a rope)

cache—a deposit of food or equipment stored for later use

climbing rope—used here to describe a 150-foot nylon rope, nine millimeters (about one-third-inch) thick, used by one climber to prevent the other from falling far in the event of a slip

cornice—used here to mean an overhanging lip of snow, formed by wind, and likely to slice away if disturbed

couloir—a large gully or gorge in a mountain face

crampons—spikes attached to the boot that enable a climber to ascend steep ice or snow

crevasse—a split, crack, or narrow opening in a glacier

dehydrate—to lose too much water or body fluids; climbers often have this condition at high altitudes where the air is extremely dry

face—used here to describe an exposed surface of rock, ice, or snow on a mountain

glacier—a large body of ice moving slowly down a mountain slope or valley or spreading out on a land surface

Gore-tex—the brand name of a material that allows air to pass through, but not water; it is used to make lightweight, waterproof clothing

ice ax—a tool used by climbers to secure holds on ice; an ice ax has a long shaft and a head with a pick at one end

Koflak—the brand name of a popular high altitude climbing boot

lamasery—a place where lamas, or Tibetan monks, live and practice their Buddhist religion

lug sole—a special sole, or bottom part, of a boot or shoe with fittings extending beneath it

Marmot Taku—the brand name of a high altitude tent used on the Gongga Shan expedition

monsoon—used here to mean summer rains and storms which come from the southeast and blow over the Himalayas

moraine—the line of rock and gravel formed at the side or end of a glacier

overboots—cloth boots which are worn over climbing boots at high altitudes to keep out snow and keep feet warm

protocol—used here to describe the written document that recorded the agreements made by the American team with the Chinese Mountaineering Association for a climbing expedition in China

spindrift—wind-blown snow

traverse—a curving or zigzag route that marks the easiest path up a steep grade or mountain slope

wand—used here to mean a bamboo stake that climbers place in snow to mark the route they are taking

Place Names

Beijing (Peking)—the capital of China

Chengtu—a major city in China and the capital of the province of Szechwan

Gongga Shan—the name of the mountain climbed by the 1982 American expedition; it is also known as *Minya Konka*

Himalayas—the great range of high mountains which stretches across southern Asia from Afghanistan to China and includes Mount Everest, the world's highest mountain

Kangding—a city in China inhabited mainly by Tibetans

Liu Baxiang—the last town on the road to Gongga Shan

Minya Konka—another, older name for Gongga Shan

Szechwan—a province in southwestern China where Gongga Shan is located

Tibet—an autonomous region of China located in the southwestern part of the country

Xian—a major city and former capital of China, located on the rail line between Beijing and Chengtu

Yangtze—one of China's major rivers

Yellow River—a major river of China

Suggested Reading

Emmons, Arthur B., et.al. *Men above the Clouds*. Seattle: The Mountaineers, 1980. The fascinating tale of the first ascent of Gongga Shan by four young men—Burdsall, Emmons, Moore and Young—who set off to cross China by land in 1932 in "search for a mountain higher than Everest."

Herzog, Maurice. *Anannapurna*. New York: E.P. Dutton, 1953. The engrossing account of the first ascent of an 8,000-meter peak by a renowned French climber. One of the classic mountaineering books.

Ullman, James Ramsey. *The Age of Mountaineering*. New York: Lippincott, 1964. The story of mountaineering told by one of the early and best-known writers on the subject.

Unsworth, Walt. *Everest*. New York: Penguin Books, 1982. A history, not only of the skill and endurance of the climbers, but also of the international rivalry and the politics that surrounded many of the expeditions to the world's highest mountain.

Index